C000186579

The CONTENTED *Little* HUSBAND

SAY GOODBYE TO TEMPER TANTRUMS AND UNHELPFUL HABITS

Tess Read

First published in Great Britain in 2016 by
Michael O'Mara Books Limited
9 Lion Yard
Tremadoc Road
London SW4 7NQ

A CIP catalogue record for this book is available
from the British Library.

Papers used by Michael O'Mara Books Limited are natural,
recyclable products made from wood grown in sustainable forests.
The manufacturing processes conform to the environmental
regulations of the country of origin.

ISBN: 978-1-78243-603-4 in hardback print format

1 2 3 4 5 6 7 8 9 10

Designed and typeset by Jade Wheaton
Illustrations by Andrew Pinder
Cover illustration by Greg Stevenson

Printed and bound by CPI Group (UK) Ltd, Croydon, CR0 4YY

www.mombooks.com

Contents

To my darling husband,
Danny – of course!

INTRODUCTION

What is a Contented Little Husband?

This book addresses a very real problem in our modern world. If it doesn't afflict you personally, then I am sure you have a friend or five who has been struck down by it. This is the scenario: lovely attentive boyfriend proposes to you, you marry and settle down in a haze of wedded bliss. Then something happens. He changes. Specifically, he regresses. He turns from being a fully functioning adult who is able to cook, wash and clean for himself to something a little different. To something a little more, well, helpless.

All too soon after you settle into your marital home, he

begins no longer to wash his own clothes; you are cooking more and more of the meals; you are buying presents for his family ... And suddenly there you are – not so much his beloved wife, but more like – dare we say it – his mother. Yes, it is almost as if those wedding bells have turned your lovely man into a helpless, somewhat useless infant.

What to do? You may not realize it but you hold the power to lovingly educate your darling boy. With great power comes great responsibility, and your responsibility here is heavy. He may no longer have the ability to look after himself properly; he needs you to teach him how to be an adult again. You need to make sure he never lets you down with infantile behaviour or uncalled-for tantrums. Above all, you need to teach him how to be a good husband and what that really means. As in most things, we must share some of the blame ourselves – perhaps you spoiled him a little at first? Picked his clothes up off the floor, washed them even and returned them to him in a neat pile at the foot of the bed, signifying your womanly love? Does this sound familiar? Remember, spare the rod and spoil the child; or to put it another way: wash and fold his clothes for him once and you will face a lifetime of sorting through his festering pile of dirty underwear. Did you sign up for this in your wedding vows? You did not.

It is your responsibility to educate him properly so that he can function independently as a grown-up male. Fear not, I am with you all the way. I am here to help you in this long and arduous journey to help your gorgeous boy grow back into an almost functioning adult. We want to make sure you never go out of an evening and return to a house so thoroughly ransacked that you are sure you have had burglars, only to find that husband has done the damage as he searched fruitlessly for the tin opener, and is now lying on the floor near a half-opened tin of Spam sobbing gently. You can just hear him intoning these words under his breath, like an incantation: 'She's moved the tin opener again. I left it on the side where I knew where it was. Why does she always move things? Why? Why?'

It would be funny if it weren't so tragic.

So we must not let this happen. We will start by looking at how to create the ideal home environment for your darling one. Then, using my years of experience, I have developed the vital Contented routines. Although your boy is most certainly an individual, unique in this world and entirely without parallel, he shares with all his fellow men the desperate need for a routine: almost like a child he needs the grown-up equivalent of being put down for a sleep. You may find that left to his own devices he will watch sporting event after sporting event, but in fact he also requires quiet time, which you may have to enforce (it is often useful to keep a stack of car magazines handy for this purpose).

He also needs a routine around eating – he needs you to guide him towards the understanding that there are three meals in every day, not just show-off dinner-party food to be produced by him with a flourish, but all the everyday meals too, preferably not always cooked by you. We will look at how to get feeding right, and will turn our attention to the tricky subject of weaning ... weaning him off unsuitable friends, language and interests, that is.

Planning is always vital when it comes to your darling boy. For example, for his first Christmas, you really must have a plan to prevent you becoming Mother Christmas to all his family as well as your own. Instead of this nightmare scenario, you can give him back that most precious gift – the gift of giving.

An often thorny subject is toilet training, above all training him in putting down the loo seat. A seemingly impossible ask, but I assure you it can be achieved. Once he has mastered this skill, you can move on to advanced toilet training – the holy grails of putting down the loo lid, and even washing hands afterwards. This can be a tricky one for your darling to learn, and requires a lot of patience and tact on your part, but will be well worth the effort.

We will then discover strategies and tactics for encouraging him in the hardest task of all – asking for directions without having a tantrum. This proficiency will especially come in handy when on holiday, and I'll also share my experience of how gentle guidance can make sure you get the holiday you want (expensive and nice) and not the holiday he wants (cheap and grotty).

Worried wives around the world have written to me about the debilitating condition that is man flu, and I will reveal how to understand it, with advice on how to fake sympathy and get your big baby to grow up and get over it.

By these means and many more, through this book you have the chance to give your lovely boy his independence back. Your husband will become a Contented husband – aware of his duties and responsibilities, such as taking out the bins and cooking lunch as well as a fancy meal at Christmas. And you can find out how to put shelves up and pictures on the walls so that you never, ever, have to 'nag' him to do it. Contented husband, Contented you.

Over the years, many women have contacted me to offer their thanks for the difference that my humble work has made to their lives. Here is a short selection of their kind words in praise of the Contented Little Husband method.

'I cannot express my gratitude for your incredible ideas and routines strongly enough. Since I read your book and started my gorgeous boy on your routines nine months ago, I now have a happy, helpful man about the house. Whenever anyone comes to the house he immediately offers them refreshments without me having to suggest it, let alone do it myself. He always puts the loo seat down and never forgets my birthday. Everyone remarks – within earshot – on what a Contented Little Husband he is. He just smiles weakly and goes back to the ironing.'

'I read about the ideas for a Contented Little Husband and so, as soon as I decided Mike was marriage material, I tried out the routines and they worked a treat. Since then he has never really been too much of a handful. All my friends are obscenely jealous!'

'Thank you for everything. Your book should be nominated for a Nobel Peace Prize – it certainly kept the peace in our house! No more arguments about whose job it is to unload the dishwasher – it's always his! Fabulous.'

'Thank you so much for your amazing book – it has revolutionized my life. It is no exaggeration to say that it is the single most important text that I have ever read in my entire life.'

1

PREPARING FOR THE
NEW ARRIVAL

*Creating a home for your
bundle of joy*

In an ideal world, once you are sharing your home with your
special new person, your amazing bundle of joy, you want to
have everything set up for him to enjoy his new surroundings
in just the right way. For him to grow as a person there are
certain things that he really needs. I am not talking about
themed wallpaper or matching furniture – you may like these
things, but there is no chance he will appreciate them. Yes,
he needs storage solutions, but not the ones you find in the

designer magazines in colour-coordinated ranges. We are not talking stacking storage with built-in dimmable lights.

Instead, it's a man shed you need to be creating, or a man drawer if budgets are tight.

GETTING READY FOR THE BIG DAY

The day when you bring your darling home from the hospital (or, more likely, the pub) and settle him into your home is a big, exciting day! It's all too easy to get caught up in the excitement of the moment and concentrate on the certainly very important issues such as feeding and sleeping, to the detriment of other things that are just as important. Just as you need a space to simply *be* in your shared home – the living room with glass of wine in hand and the television on most probably – so does he. But whereas you may only need a bottle of Shiraz, *Homeland* on TV and Facebook on the iPad, he needs a little more. And it's your job to prepare for that big day by getting the home ready for this new arrival. He needs a place to be, too, and he needs things in that place. He is a bear and he needs a cave. He needs to fulfil his ancient primeval instincts.

And for a really happy bear, stock it well with all those things a bear needs – beer, batteries, unidentified cables and a mountain of total and utter junk.

CREATING HIS OWN SHED?

Many men delight in creating their own man shed. They may regard it as a project over time to build up just the right level of useless dud batteries happily mingling with fresh new batteries in a way in which no one can ever tell which is which. They may enjoy collecting the pointless cables of dead bits of random electronica that no one will ever use ever again and stuffing them into boxes too small for them, or just leaving them strewn all over the floor. However, you may not like the associated expense that this process involves – the constant buying of new electronics and cables to connect them to the old. Plus, you are unlikely to enjoy the resultant storage implications of never throwing away anything ever that might one day allegedly be slightly useful for some unidentified task. And finally, his choice of location for this man shed may not be desirable. After all, you were planning to turn that alcove in the bedroom into a walk-in wardrobe for yourself.

So, what is the solution? To create the man shed for him, of course! If you have an actual shed in the garden, then of course use that. If not, then second best is a small room in the house for him to have to himself – it doesn't matter if it's the one where the radiator doesn't work and even the woodworm has woodworm. Your darling boy won't care. And if he does, well – he can do a spot of DIY and do something about it, right? If none of these are an option, then a drawer at the bottom of his chest of drawers will suffice. Once you've chosen the location then all that remains is, like a piñata, to fill it!

WHAT'S IN A MAN SHED?

To the untrained eye the contents of a man shed appear to be nothing but crud. Random, useless crud. But the point is that it is always 'potentially useful' crud, and it is *his* crud. A good man shed has booze in it too.

If space allows, start with a small fridge, and put a few beers in it. This token of your affection for him will go a

long way to him forgiving you for turning the alcove in the bedroom into your walk-in wardrobe in exchange for this fabulous man shed you are creating somewhere far less desirable. Then add a chair – you can put in that rubbish one that you got for free at a conference that he's always said you both should take on a camping trip, and that you've always wanted to get rid of. Then, if possible, add one more bit of furniture – a bookcase or similar. Onto this should go a colourful collection of cables, phones and music players that 'might still work if you fancied taking them apart', an assortment of batteries which you can claim 'mostly work', maybe a book or two about his favourite subject, and lastly all the *objets d'art* from round the house that you don't like, such as the little statue of an elephant he brought back from Thailand, or the shells he collected from a beach on holiday with a previous girlfriend.

All of this effort on your part shows a commendable degree of thoughtfulness towards the light of your life. A further practical effect is that you are managing to declutter the house of all those tasteless bits of tat he likes.

From then on he can claim whenever he retreats to his man shed that he is 'going to have one beer followed by a go at fixing a few things', while we all know he is going to have one beer followed by another beer followed by not really fixing anything. And you can claim that you know how important it is for everyone to have their space to do their own thing, and that you really respect his hobbies.

Result!

Don't be tempted to just chuck away the useless cables, whatever you do: you will never hear the end of it. Don't forget the well-known saying: 'Thy man shed is thy cave providing thou hast stuffed it with useless bits of dead electronica along with a few old copies of *Private Eye*.'

2

EARLY DAYS

Putting him into a routine

WHY HAVE A ROUTINE?

I know how it is. Here comes that first day when you bring your little tyke home and discover all that extra paraphernalia that comes with him – you never knew he would come with so much baggage! And you don't want to restrict him. You don't want to tie him down with ideas of dreaded 'routines'.

Who needs four-hourly feeding? you think to yourself. We can just wing it, right? We can be spontaneous, why not? Have lunch when we feel like it, dinner *if* we feel like it. Some days when he gets back from work you can make *him* a gin and tonic, and some days he will fetch *you* a glass of wine, and it's all good. It's all mutual and grown-up and shared, and it's all your own ways of being. You two together have created your own ways of being with each other, of learning about each other and choosing how your lives will be. And what could be better than that? Why would you need a routine? You are an independent free spirit; your relationship is strong and built on mutual trust and love. Routines? Pah! You spit in their face. Right?

As the famous novelist Honoré de Balzac said, 'Marriage must constantly fight against a monster which devours everything: routine.'

Balzac certainly lived by his word – eschewing the dreaded routine of matrimonial life in favour of a decades-long love-letter affair with a Polish countess whom he finally married in his fifties after eighteen years and a final ten-hour back-breaking carriage journey in Ukraine, only to die just five months later.

Which rather leads one to think that he may not have been the best agony uncle. We may need to look for advice elsewhere. Let us take a leaf out of that Great Briton Winston Churchill's book. Did he believe in routine? He surely did.

His routine was a simple one. He woke early, as all God-fearing people do, at 7.30 a.m. And then stayed in bed for several hours reading the news, dictating to secretaries and eating a gargantuan breakfast. He then rose and began his first whisky and soda. A lunch soon followed accompanied by healthy doses of champagne, succeeded by a working afternoon before some more whisky and sodas and his mid-afternoon siesta. This was followed by a several-course dinner before a final hour or so of work.

And he won a world war, was prime minister twice and wrote over fifty books. So, if that's good enough for him ...

CRAVING FOR A ROUTINE

And thus we bring things back to our modern-day domestic situations. Here the crucial fact of the matter is that you love your darling boy, and he really *is* a darling boy! He is perfect in so many ways: he makes you feel good when your single friends complain about dating, you have someone to go out with on Valentine's Day ... I could go on and on. But when he is tired, perfect he is not. When he is hungry, delightful company he isn't. And it's all too easy for him to become overtired and desperately hungry if you aren't there to take care of him. You know only too well how capable he is of fooling around for hours with his latest toys without a thought for his need for sleep or food if you don't stop him. He might think that what he wants is unlimited playtime with his latest electronic toy, or curating his playlists, but really what he craves, deep down inside, is a routine.

THE ROUTINE

Now, I'm not saying that one size fits all. Of course, we are all different. And your lovely boy is no exception. But one size does in fact completely fit all in this instance. He may think he's special and different, but when it comes to which routine is needed, there's just one. And here's the secret to a Contented Little Husband: there are just two essential elements to the routine. Firstly, if you were to compare matters to, for example, a childcare book, every time you read about putting your bundle of joy down for a sleep, translate this into letting him have some delimited mindless time playing a video game or on Twitter. And secondly, every time those books talk about your darling one wanting to feed, well, that translates to a nice cold beer.

That's it! I know – easy-peasy, right?

Do be aware that it is essential to allow the mindless

quiet time – you may even need to enforce it. It is vital that your special boy spends some time occupied with his own thoughts or other such mindless things, rather than you. He needs to feel the contrast to know how to appreciate you when you are around.

As for how often he should have a beer – once every four hours should be enough.

PERFECTING THE ROUTINE

Of course, you can gradually add a few other elements to the routine. For example, when you go out to see your friends he has to cook for himself *and* clean the kitchen afterwards rather than leave it as a ghastly mess for you to come back to. Plus, you'll want to be getting him doing those really tedious household things like sorting out the parking tickets straight away, rather than just saying he is going to do it, missing the deadline, paying the higher amount and hiding this from you. And a few other bits and pieces – like it's a good idea to make him responsible for all gardening (unless you like gardening, of course), as well as things like being responsible for ironing his own shirts. The possibilities are

endless. But these are just details to be added to the main cornerstones of the routine.

It is important that he feels he has options in the routine (even if that isn't, strictly speaking, true), and that he has ownership over them. So, to achieve this effect it helps to add one element at a time so that he feels in control. This way he will simply get on with the next element, while at the same time feeling that it is something he has *chosen* to do. He will also begin to feel a key benefit of the routine – it will make him feel safe and eliminate his fear of the unknown. And meanwhile, you will have a Contented Little Husband happy in the house and garden doing the chores, and that's got to be good for you – and will eliminate *your* fear of having to do these things yourself.

With your special boy in a routine you will have time for all the things that are so important to you but you were never able to find time for before. J. K. Rowling famously wrote the first *Harry Potter* books when her little angel was having her daily naps. So, no excuses.

Routine and roles around the home

Now that you have fixed his daily routine in terms of his hunger/tired cycle, it's time to move onto the next phase of your married routine – that is to say, working out who is responsible for doing what around your house.

So what is it that he expects you to do around the house? Let's see, it's the cooking, the cleaning, the washing ... Oh, and let's not forget that now that we're emancipated and all we get to go out to work too! Jolly good. As Joan Collins said, 'We should celebrate being women and having the opportunities to do things that our mothers and grandmothers were not allowed to do. They were expected to stay at home and do the cooking and the cleaning. Though now, of course, we are expected to do the cooking and the cleaning *and* the working.'

Well, quite. Research shows that women are still doing two-thirds of the housework, even in houses where they are the main breadwinner. That can't be right, can it? Factually right, but morally wrong, no? So where did these households go awry? The problem is simple – a lack of routine.

Without routine your darling boy will never settle into the sort of Contented Little Husband you want to be living with. To keep him a happy soul we have already seen that he needs good sleep patterns, established eating patterns, lots of beer and he also needs to know what is expected of him. He can't always throw his toys out of the pram and expect you to pick them up!

GREAT EXPECTATIONS

So what is it that you expect him to do around the house? DIY, the bins … Er, that's it?

That's not enough. You need to set your standards higher, and set your expectation levels above the barest minimum. Believe in him. He can do more!

What does he *like* doing around the house? DIY. Why does he like it? Because it's actually often quite fun. And it's also a high-status activity: 'Look at those shelves I put up! It took ages and was really difficult, you wouldn't understand how it's done.' What else does he like doing? Getting the big fancy BBQ going and cooking on it when a bunch of friends come over, yes? And cooking the Christmas dinner, which takes about seventy-two hours and uses every single dish in the house (the show-off cooking, in other words)?

What does he *not* like doing? The cleaning, the washing, the vacuuming ... What do you not like doing? Guess what – it's the same stuff! So, the obvious question is, why is it that even though we don't like doing these things any more than he does, mostly we are doing them?

Is this what we want? I think not. What do we want instead? Here I will call upon one of my army of loyal followers to outline the dream scenario:

'I believe that we have found the secret of a happy marriage. He cooks, he cleans, he loads the washing machine and folds the clothes ... and I make the bed! It's perfect!'

YOUR SACRIFICE

Yes, I am afraid you have to give something up. Everyone must make sacrifices to make a relationship work. Everyone has to play their part. You have to accept, and willingly so, your allotted task: you have to make the bed, each morning.

This is a task you have to take on happily and throw your soul into. Stretch out that sheet! Smooth out that duvet! Plump up those pillows and arrange those occasional cushions. Hell, you can even go crazy here and pull a bedspread across the whole damn shooting match and really make your bedroom look like a dodgy hotel if you like. What's important is that it gets done, and it's you who does it. Then each morning as you go into the kitchen for breakfast, and the question of who is to cook/clean/wash what today emerges as a huge, great, massive elephant in the room ... you know that your conscience is clear.

You made the bed. You have done your bit.

STAGE ONE: WHIZZ AROUND THE KITCHEN

So now it's his turn. Breakfast? Well, you can both get your own bits for breakfast, right? No need for anyone to wait on anyone else here. Even stacking the dishwasher is clearly a task for each of you for your own dishes. No issues. Then comes the small amount of kitchen cleaning that needs to be done afterwards. For this I advise the casual: 'Are you OK to whizz a cloth around the kitchen, darling, so that it's all sorted?' It could be this is his first acquaintance with the concept of kitchen cleaning, so you may have to put up with a pretty poor result, and indeed a pretty shocked expression on his face, but let the question hang there nevertheless. If there is a short pause, be sure to follow this up with: 'I've made the bed.' Chances are, whether due to his dazed state or well-meaning character, he will attempt some basic cleaning.

Excellent. This is stage one. Do not on any account skip this stage, it is vital to success.

Now comes stage two. What about all those DIY tasks that need doing? Those shelves that need to be put up, or those banisters that need to be painted? Or that mirror that has been sitting on the floor waiting for him to have 'a moment' to put it up? What about if you started doing all these things? What about if you did the DIY, then wouldn't he have to put the washing on?

Yes, I rather think he would.

STAGE TWO: THE OLD SWITCHEROO

So here comes the clever bit. You take on a bunch of DIY tasks – don't worry, they're really not hard (see chapter on Common Problems Solved for advice and handy hints).

Then you can start checking the oil in the car and doing other basic car maintenance too. So now what are the extra bits that he needs to do around the house to be pulling his weight? Suddenly you are painting the gloss on the front door when all that washing needs to be done. What to do? Paintbrush in hand, dust sheets on the floor, you call out to your beloved something along the following lines:

> *'Darling, I think I'll be another hour or so on this door
> – would you mind putting a wash on please? I usually
> use programme X but the instruction manual is on top
> of the machine if you want to have a look. Thanks!'*

Having the instruction manual handy by the machine is vital to success – he doesn't want to have to admit he has no idea how your joint washing machine works and that he has never before had to operate it, and he certainly doesn't want to just have to follow your direction about the 'best' programme. But he can read instruction manuals for complicated machinery – of course he can – so now he can spend a happy twenty minutes figuring out where to put the powder and establishing that programme X is probably the 'easiest' option but that programme Y should be considered in certain circumstances, which is of course obvious nonsense but there's no need to pick him up on this.

Next moment you are to be seen elbows deep in the car's bonnet, checking the dipstick for well-oiledness or otherwise, and again you cheerfully call out:

You: 'Darling, I'm just going to pop to the garage to buy more oil for the car, it's running low again. I'll only be about half an hour. Do you mind just giving the kitchen a quick once over while I'm gone so we can have a nice lunch when we're back?'

Him: 'Errrr, OK. Are you sure you wouldn't rather leave it to me?'

You: 'No, no, it's no problem. I have a loyalty card for the garage anyway so I get a discount there. I'll see you in a bit!'

The loyalty card is a great wheeze – he knows he has never taken one out, so now you're saving the household money, and that is purely irresistible.

Then you finish with the masterstroke:

You: 'Oh, just a thought. We'll probably both be hungry by the time I get back, so could you pop something on for lunch, please? Perhaps you could try that new recipe that we [be sure to use 'we' here, not 'I'] spotted the other day? You're so great at new recipes! Must be off now, see you later!'

Him: 'Er, OK, darling, see you soon.'

And so you have done it. Contented Little Husband goes into the house and whips you up a storm in the kitchen while you pop up the high street for a saunter around the shops – the car has obviously not run out of oil again that quickly.

KEEP GOING – DON'T LOSE HEART!

So, all you have to do now is keep this sort of behaviour up all day every weekend, come rain or shine, and you will have him doing the everyday cooking, the cleaning … in short, all those dreaded household chores that have so eloquently, and now happily inaccurately, been called Women's Work. Not any more – now it's Contented Little Husband's work.

So now your house will radiate contentment as he cleans the kitchen, vacuums the sitting room, cooks dinner and whips up G & Ts for guests as soon as they walk in the door. After all, you did make the bed. Congratulations. You have a Contented routine – for him, and especially for you!

NO ONE LIKES DOING THE BINS

Oh yes. And it's still his job to do the bins, whether he likes it or not.

> ### Top Tip
>
> Things not to say: 'It's so lovely that we're such a modern household, with you being the one who's barefoot and pregnant in the kitchen. I would say "without the pregnant bit", but having seen the beer belly you're growing, I'm not so sure!'

And so to bed

I get it. I see what you're like. You turned straight to this chapter, didn't you? Admit it, you did. Fine, OK, so here it is. The simple truth of how to keep your husband Contented in the bedroom. It's a short chapter, but it contains several ultimate kernels of truth. I don't think you'll be disappointed.

Again, as with so much of life surrounding your darling one, guess what – it's all about a routine, of course! In this case a bedtime routine. I mean, sex on the living-room floor or in the kitchen is all very well, but carpet burns and breadcrumbs can be such a hazard that it's far better to have a proper bedtime routine.

The difficulty is that, especially in the early days, your angel may have trouble settling to sleep, and may also be unable to sleep a whole night through without disturbing you one or more times. As in the classic joke: he slept like a baby, which is to say he woke up every few hours crying. This kind of lack of sleep is no good for anyone, so we need to nip it in the bud right now. Fear not, the Contented routine is here to help.

A BEDTIME STORY

As with small children, a key element of the bedtime routine is the bedtime story. And as with small children, a bit of repetition here is no bad thing. At some point in their development, small children will crave being told the same story again and again, night after night. Your own darling boy is no different. But in his case it isn't so much a story about a talking elephant or a refugee bear stowaway that will do the job. It's true you need to use your imagination: you need to weave a wonderfully crafted tale of fantasy. But this fantasy is one that will appeal to virtually every husband, as it will offer them tantalizing thrills of potential future contentment. What you do is tell him a long, repetitive story about how you are going to have sex with him another night. Simples. Then, as with small children, let him drop off to sleep by himself, while you get a full night's beauty sleep or even kick back with a bottle of wine, a box of chocolates and your *Bridesmaids* DVD in a happy fog of contentment.

CONTENTED? REALLY?

Now, you may be concerned that this solution doesn't actually create a Contented husband, or even a Contented you. And you may not be entirely happy with the formula of letting him go to bed alone while you're in another room with the telly on (even if *Bridesmaids* is a classic). But trust me, this is the only way for him to relearn how to go to sleep by himself, and indeed to remember how to sleep through the night, and so let you do the same.

You may also worry that this routine could leave him, and possibly also you, actually rather miserable, such that you

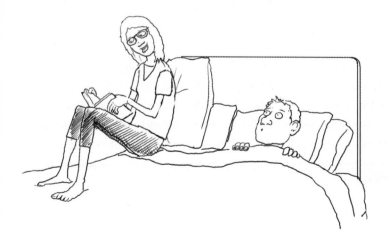

both end up looking for happiness elsewhere and that could lead to no kind of contentment for anyone (unless you're a divorce lawyer, of course, in which case it could lead to a new house in the country). Well, all I can say to that is that this is not the kind of self-help book that says you should look after your husband in the bedroom and keep him happy or he will look for satisfaction elsewhere – no siree! Rather, this is the kind of self-help book that says if you don't bother me with details about your sex life, I won't bother you with mine. OK?

As the saying goes: don't tell people your problems because 80 per cent of them won't care, and the other 20 per cent will celebrate.

GO CRAZY – DITCH THE ROUTINE!

Now this is really crazy talk, right? I've just explained the importance of routines! But sometimes it's actually a good idea to shake things up in the bedroom. Just as when a small child is in the routine of waking up at 5 a.m. or earlier and not going back to sleep, something the child-rearing books don't tell you is that one way you can try to get them to ditch the habit is by keeping them up super late every night until their little systems are so confused they will do anything for a lie-in. In a similar way, sometimes you and your darling boy deserve a shake-up in the bedroom.

This is always a particularly good idea when you need him in a good mood so he'll agree to the two of you spending money on something you want that he doesn't (such as getting a builder in to do the bits of DIY that he has been promising to do for over a year).

It's also a good idea when you are about to meet up with your girlfriends in the next few days and don't want to have to admit when the subject comes up that you haven't had sex for ages. Of course, if any of them have been round to your house recently and seen the unfinished DIY work, they will already have concluded that.

PLAY GAMES IN THE BEDROOM

And I do mean Scrabble. Pictionary is also good. And personally, I say you can't beat a good game of Connect 4.

COSMO

Look, if you want more advice about your sex life then read *Cosmo* or something. I repeat that this is not a book about how to keep your husband contented in the bedroom in that kind of way. Is that all you thought this book was? Shame on you.

It's about so, so much less than that.

Progress report

By this point, your Contented Little Husband should be able to:

✓ Cook for himself without being reminded

✓ Recognize what a washing machine is and how it works

✓ Clean the house without having a tantrum

✓ Sleep through the night without disturbing you

3

GETTING TO KNOW YOU

Getting feeding right

This is such a thorny subject that there are enough books on this topic alone to take up entire shelves in bookshops. Most of them run along the following lines:

When is your gorgeous bundle of joy ready to move from mere drinking on to solids, and what are the telltale signs?

When he is ready, how do you introduce the concept of regular mealtimes without putting him off the whole process?

TIME AWAY FROM THE PUB?

In my opinion, the most important telltale sign that your boy is ready to move beyond fluids is that he is capable of enjoying time away from the pub. Is he able to spend more than two evenings in a row with you without making it increasingly obvious that he is getting restless for an evening with his mates and four hours of solid drinking and no dinner? If so, this is the best sign there could be that he may be ready to move on from drinks to solids. He may even be ready to move on to domestic kitchen happiness and in-house food production, i.e. cooking.

Dinner may be a delicious three-course meal that he has slaved over for several hours, leaving work early to fricassée the meat and sweat the shallots. Or it may be a chicken breast blackened and charred somewhat beyond perfection with an accompaniment of lukewarm, manky pasta. As long as it's not a ready meal – praise, praise, praise! Even if it is a ready meal, you should probably praise it unless you want to be cooking for the two of you every mealtime forever more.

By praising his every attempt at culinary action, you can begin to hope that you are setting him on a happy path to the future – where you feed his ego and he feeds you.

MAINTAINING REGULAR MEALTIMES

But there is a stumbling block, and that is how to maintain regular mealtimes. We all know the scenario: your lovely boy is now right in the habit of cooking for certain occasions – Christmas, obviously, but also special events such as dinner parties, barbecues etc. (essentially anything that involves an admiring audience). Now that's all very well, but we do actually need to eat a little more often than once in a blue moon – three times a day, usually. But this may be a struggle to get into your little darling's head. He appears to have no thought that the whole process will have to be repeated in a few hours' time, and then again the next day, and the day after that.

FAIL TO PLAN? OR PLAN NOT TO FAIL

I have found that a simple kitchen planner calendar can help with this. You know the type I mean, the one with the dates on it and spaces for each person to write their activities. Make sure you buy one with a lot of space for each day, and then on each weekend day or other days when you are both not out at work, write 'breakfast', 'lunch' and 'dinner'. The idea of this is *not* to tie him down to when he will cook and when you will – that route leads to disaster! He may never wield a wooden spoon again if you try to make him 'commit' in this way. No, no, the point of this is merely to set down that there are three such meals in each of the days, just to bring it subtly to his attention.

Then choose a day when neither of you have anything planned, and try this out:

You: *'I'm thinking of meeting X for tea, or should I meet them for lunch and you sort out something for lunch just for you?'*

He won't want to sort something out for lunch just for him, as that route leads to no lunch at all, and instead when you return at 4 p.m. the light of your life will be mumbling incoherently, clutching his stomach and chewing on assorted bits of brown cardboard for sustenance, unclear how he is going to make it through to the next day.

So he replies: *'No, that's fine. You meet X for tea and we can have lunch together.'*

You: *'OK, fine. I've bought those kebab things that you* *enjoy cooking but that I always seem to burn. We could have those?'*

'Of course, darling,' he replies, smiling self-indulgently at your foolish inability to look after yourself, and bingo! You have tied him down to cooking without him realizing. By introducing the subject of lunch together in this roundabout way, you have avoided a direct confrontation and led him towards your desired goal – i.e. making him remember that meals don't appear by magic – far more artfully.

Repeat with dinner, and on subsequent days, and finally you may realize your dream and never have to cook again.

THE ETERNAL EQUATION: $C + CUA = S^2$

But then we have the stumbling block that's not often mentioned in the tomes on getting feeding right, and that is the very sticky subject of: who does the clearing-up afterwards? This moral maze has a close ally with the eternal question of: why when he cooks does he have to use every single kitchen implement?

If the answer to the first question is you, then the second question has even more importance. So, this is your best hope to make the answer to the first question at least *sometimes* him, even if realistically it will need to be you most of the time. The only way I have ever heard of this being achieved is in the following way:

You: *'Thanks so much for another amazing meal, darling. Who knew that chicory and chocolate could be so delicious?'*

Him: *'Oh, you're too kind. You're a very good cook too, you know!'*

You: *[Laughing] 'That's not true – I'm nothing like as good as you! But anyway, how about you sort out the kitchen while I go and change into something more comfortable and I'll meet you upstairs in the bedroom in about, well, let's think … It will probably take at least twenty minutes to clear up, especially with all those pots and pans you used! So, plus a bit of soaking time … See you up there in half an hour? Can't wait!'*

Him: *'It's a deal, you naughty thing.'*

Little has he noticed you really have been the naughty one: dinner cooked for you and then cleared away afterwards! Seriously? You rule.

Oh, the meaning of C + CUA = S^2? Cooking plus clearing up afterwards = sex squared, obviously.

Food folklore has it that a child has to try a new food nineteen times before they should be allowed to give a verdict that they don't like it. Husbands usually take a little less. If you have tried the 'What shall we cook for lunch?' trick, say, ten times and it hasn't worked, it's time to give up. It's that or become a psychopath, and we wouldn't want that.

Toilet training

So, the time has come. Your lovely boy has been in your life for perhaps a year now. You and he have been sharing your home and sharing your life. And, crucially, sharing the bathroom. You tell him you love him every day, you give him a thousand kisses on his soft downy hair and little bald patch. But yet there is still one thing it is so hard to say: 'Why the hell can't you put the loo seat down after you wee all round it?!'

Now, this straightforward approach to the universal problem is unlikely to work, unless what you are after is a stand-up row. So, instead, to convert our bundles of joy into fully toilet-trained grown-up boys who you can reliably take to a friend's house without fear of embarrassing loo-seat-left-up incidents, follow the Contented advice on toilet training below.

COMMON QUESTIONS

Q: Why does my husband insist on leaving the toilet seat up? Does he not love me?

Now, you need to bear in mind that your boy has genuinely not yet learned that he should be toilet-trained. Maybe you are his first proper relationship, his first real love. Or maybe, shock horror, none of his previous loves had read *The Contented Little Husband* and didn't even attempt to properly toilet-train him! Whichever is the case, the fact of the matter is that he sees nothing wrong with leaving the loo seat up, and however hard this is to believe, he is really not doing it just to annoy you. So, he needs your sympathy and guidance, not annoyance at his obvious failings.

Q: How do I know when he's ready for toilet training? It seems quite early in his development.

Toilet training is, as we know, a tricky subject and it's important that you don't run before you can walk and attempt this too early on. There are two main signs that he's ready:

1. He's reached that wonderful stage of understanding his body's needs and how to control them, i.e. he no longer burps at will at family gatherings and then giggles like an infant afterwards. If he is still showing this unsavoury behaviour then I'm afraid he is not yet ready.

2. He has an awareness of correct toilet language. He knows that it's polite to say things like 'I'm just going to the loo, I'll be back in a minute,' rather than 'Just going for slash.' If not, then you'll need more work on him before you can introduce toilet training.

If he has an awareness of correct toilet language and of bodily needs and how to control them, and has possibly even reached the level of understanding that when a toilet roll runs out a new one needs to be put out straight away then – hooray! – he is ready for toilet training.

Q: **Can't I just tell him how much it annoys me and ask him to put the seat down?**

I have heard of approaches to toilet training that have us believe that it is possible to simply show your boy the toilet and explain why it is much nicer for you if he would please put the loo seat down in future. A shorthand way of describing this approach is of 'appealing to his good nature'. I laugh in the face of such absurdity, and if you had had to train as many boys on the toilet as I have, so would you. Feel free to try this method, but bear in mind that unless you are very lucky, it has very little hope of working and is more likely to result in stubborn rebellion.

Q: **Why is his aim so bad? Is there something wrong with him?**

Boys love having something to shoot at, right? So, why is it that their wee so often fails to hit the mark? The answer is usually simple: lack of practice, which itself stems from a lack of *permission* to practise, going right back to infanthood. So you need to give your boy that permission.

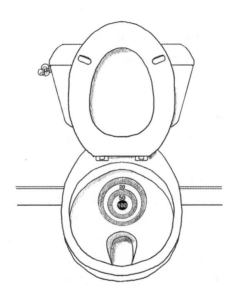

Begin by discussing the situation openly. Tell him how amazing it is that, because of their different physiognomy, boys are able to aim precisely and accurately, but you assume it must take practice to get it right. Right? His little eyes will light up at hearing this – have you just given him permission to practise? Yes, you have!

To quote the great Scotsman Robbie Burns, who proclaimed, 'We twa hae piddled in the burn, frae morning sun till dine,' we see that there is a long tradition of men going round urinating in streams, which we can safely assume was early Scottish target practice. Unless it was just for the hell of it, of course.

Q: **How can I get him to put the loo seat down?**

Now that he has had permission to practise he will presumably, hopefully, improve his aim. If you are lucky there will now be more urine in the toilet than out of it, which is a great thing, but we have still not made any progress to the Promised Land: a world in which the loo seat is routinely put down afterwards. But worry not, Contented readers, for this we have the rewards-based approach!

After months of pretty unpleasant fieldwork spent in bathrooms in fourteen different countries, I have formulated the simplest method of encouraging the fabled loo-seat-down behaviour we women so desperately crave. The first step is a loo seat and lid that you and your boy choose together, which is actually *his* choice. It could have his team's logo on it, it could be a boyish mixture of black and orange, it could even have the words 'Wow, you're amazing' written on it in a circle around the rim; it matters not, as long as it works. And this is how you make it work. Make sure *you* always leave the loo *lid* down, and comment on how great it looks very frequently. The loo seat is, of course, of the same design as the lid but it is less work to put it down.

The result of this is that he begins to put the loo seat down to remind himself of his great choice on which you keep commenting. And when he does this he also gets to not conform with the bathroom procedure that you appear to want, which is to say loo *lid* down. So, voila! He puts the loo seat down to admire his brilliance, and to theoretically revolt against your dictums in a teeny, tiny way.

Soon he will start putting the loo seat down and washing his hands in one seamless movement! (See page 60 for advice on encouraging handwashing.) And don't worry, once a few months of loo-seat putting-down has happened and has become habitual behaviour, you can swap back that horrid loo seat he likes for the one you like.

Q: Can I use reward stickers to get him to put the loo seat down?

I like your thinking. The classic solution for this is the simple but informative 'Put me down' sticker, which you can buy ready-printed or write yourself and put on the underside of the loo seat for him to see and act upon. But you can also try a more imaginative approach and devise stickers that appeal to his particular personality. So, if he is a classical music lover you could have 'Bach says – put it down', or if he is a golf fan it could be 'A hole in one – sit on that!' A nice one for lovers of war games, or actual warfare, is 'This seat is like a hand grenade – put it down as soon as you've finished with it'.

The aim of the stickers is partly to serve as a reminder but mostly as an embarrassment factor, which he will want to have taken off the loo as soon as possible so that guests don't see it. Stick it on with superglue so you have a chance of the lesson being learned before he scrapes it off.

Q: **I still can't get him to put the loo seat down – I've tried everything! Should I abandon all hope of ever achieving it?**

Yes. You have to face facts – your loo seat isn't going down unless you put it down. The only last recourse you·have is the 'nuclear option' but this is unsafe, unkind and possibly illegal so I will not share it with you. No, I simply refuse. Suffice it to say it involves a healthy (or should that be unhealthy?) dose of laxatives applied to his curry so that he needs the loo seat down in a hurry over a period of twenty-four hours or more. The theory is that he will now appreciate the benefit of keeping the loo seat down. But to be honest, it's a pretty weak theory, and clearly unacceptable behaviour on your part.

Just give up, already.

Top Tip

You just can't win 'em all.

Advanced toilet training

Now this is the obvious holy grail of toilet training. This is the ultimate, near impossible goal, which many say that, like the dream of supermarket queues having a sign saying 'Five items or fewer' rather than the inevitable 'Five items or less', can never be achieved within our lifetime. But, dear readers, I say we should believe in the impossible! I say we should strive to attain near unattainable goals! I say we should not run cowering away from tasks that daunt us! We should embrace them, eyes wide, ready for the challenge. We must never give up, and even when our last sinew of strength has gone, in our last breath we should still be gasping out the words, 'I believe!' Yes, belief is all! If you believe that your gorgeous boy *can* put the toilet lid down before flushing, *as well as* the seat, and then even wash his hands, then maybe, just maybe, he will.

ADVANCED TOILET TRAINING PART 1: PUTTING THE LID DOWN

We've tackled putting the seat down, now let's reach for the sky and attempt to get him to put the lid down too. Deep breath, you can do it.

In desperate times use a newspaper

No, it's not what you think. I do actually mean reading it in this case. And here's why. There is a small possibility that the darling creature in your care has heard about germs, and may even know they are bad for you. If this is the case, then your task here can begin with leaving in the bathroom an article that was recently doing the rounds in which researchers prove that putting the loo lid down before flushing greatly reduces the volume of germs in the air. Allegedly, these germs have the unsettling habit of settling on nearby surfaces and so contaminating them. I know it sounds like an excuse for bad toilet jokes, but it is honestly true. (No need to point out to your boy that putting the loo lid down is only an important germ preventer if someone actually has a virus, and that otherwise it's fairly irrelevant except that it just looks nicer that way.)

The power of promotion

If the germ approach fails to bring about any changes in behaviour, then move on to the second strategy. This is all about endorsement. For success here you need to introduce their favourite icon, and bandy their name about rather shamelessly. Be sure that whichever icon you pick is actually still flavour of the month with your chap though, otherwise the plan will no longer work. It was a sad day when my boy moved beyond Bob the Builder. Yes, we pretended it was 'our' joke, but I found Bob always got me what I wanted.

For example: 'Bob the Builder would like bathtime now.' 'Bob the Builder likes getting to my sister's house on time for lunch parties.' 'Bob the Builder wants to clean the kitchen.'

But, yes, whoever your boy's icon is – name them, and bring them into the great toilet debate. For example, find some way to weave the following into conversation, it shouldn't be that difficult:

'I hear that Tiger Woods says it's always a good idea to put the toilet lid down after flushing. Apparently he does it every time!'

Of course, be sure to use the icon of choice most likely to appeal to your boy. Tiger Woods may not be the hot topic any more, I don't keep entirely up to date with developments in sport.

The downside

There is a small chance your lovely boy will think you're mental for making this obviously false claim about Tiger Woods or some other hero of his such as Lance Armstrong. But equally, there is a small chance that he will wish to follow his hero in everything he is, however implausibly, claimed to do. The small chance of bringing about the holy grail of toilet etiquette is surely worth it for the risk of a slight increase of the amount by which he considers you to be mental.

After all, he already thinks you're bonkers for the number of handbags you own, not to mention shoes, and don't get him started on scarves. So what's a bit more crazy between friends? He already loves you.

If germs and promotion both fail

If you have tried the germ technique, and the promotion strategy, then I have just one idea left. It's not much of one, I apologize. You could try just asking him to do it, and 'appeal to his better nature'.

OK, sorry, I said it was rubbish.

ADVANCED TOILET TRAINING PART 2: HANDWASHING

Of course, handwashing is a vital part of toilet training but it is a relatively advanced step. Many boys will think, and possibly even say, 'I don't need to wash my hands after a simple urination visit because I only touched my penis and that's pretty clean.' I don't think I need to elaborate on how unacceptable this is. But I will anyway: this is *completely* unacceptable! What to do about this mindset?

The best strategy to encourage handwashing at home is to buy towels that will appeal to his humorous side, and put them in the bathroom. The one that I have found to work most effectively is the one that says 'Hands' on one side of the towel, and 'Arse' on the other. Genuinely, men of virtually every age seem to find this utterly hilarious. Then, towel in place, you say, pointedly: 'So I have bought this special towel for you to wipe your hands on, *every time* you use the toilet.' You could accompany this with 'I heard that so and so [insert sporting anti-hero who missed an easy goal recently or some such] doesn't wash his hands after going to the toilet! Urgh! Thank goodness I have you in my life, my lovely!' And then cross your fingers, a lot.

ADVANCED TOILET TRAINING PART 3: TOILET NOT SHOWER

It is a lamentable fact of modern life that many men pee in the shower. I know, it's not nice. I don't like it any more than you do. Of course it shouldn't be allowed, but how can it be prevented? The one backstop position you must have here is that, as Marge said to Homer: 'I don't mind if you pee in the shower, as long as you are actually having a shower at the time.' It's so true.

I apologize for leaving this chapter on such a bleak, sad note. My thoughts and feelings are with you all. Has your man been toilet-trained? I may never know. I am alone with my questions in the silence. All I can do is wish you luck with your quest.

Good luck, my friend.

Progress report

By this point, your Contented Little Husband should be able to:

✓ Consume proper, regular meals rather than a liquid diet

✓ Clear up after cooking without having a tantrum

✓ Put the toilet seat down

✓ Wash his hands regularly

✓ And, if you're very lucky, put the toilet lid down

4

BABY STEPS TO A CONTENTED YOU

Gifts

We all know how it goes: before you knew your young man he was a reasonably well-functioning individual. He could wash and dress himself (with varying degrees of success); he could hold down friendships; and he (mostly) remembered birthdays and the fact that Christmas is usually celebrated by the giving and, if necessary, the posting of presents. He even knew that this had to be done before the last Christmas posting date, which, to be fair, can be tricky for us all.

But the second that you come into his life, all of this

independence and his former ability to function relatively autonomously goes out of the window, and your lovely boy has been reduced back to a state of near infancy. As if by some sort of magic only conjured by matrimony, control over many aspects of his life are now in your hands, and gifts are one of the first things you'll find on your plate. But, for the sake of your own sanity, this is an element of his life that needs to remain his.

Let me reveal to you the saga of Christmas past, present and future if you let him give you the poisoned chalice that is being in charge of presents.

CHRISTMAS PAST

Each Christmas begins with lists. First there is the list of your family, for whom presents need to be bought. Plus associated hangers-on in the form of neighbours, work colleagues and friends. Perhaps your total is around fifteen Christmas presents to buy. Not forgetting husband too, of course! So sixteen. Good grief, no wonder we are all broke and exhausted by January.

Now, your husband's list is obviously not quite so long, and if he had his way would probably extend to his mum, you and, er, that's it. And he might forget you, or his mum (it could be either really, but you mustn't take this personally). However, he is aware that he cannot actually leave out brother, grandparents, aged aunts, etc. He will certainly cut out the non-essentials – 'What do you mean we need to buy a present for the neighbours?' – but it still leaves up to nine presents from him that need to be chosen, bought and delivered.

This he used to do each year before he met you, often quite badly, usually selecting overpriced things because they were bought in a mad rush with little thought taken over them, and generally late, but the job would be (sort of) done. But now, guess who is around to do it instead – muggins!

CHRISTMAS FUTURE

Here's how the conversation goes:

You: *'What shall we get for your brother/parent/aunt/niece this year for Christmas?'*

Him: *'Oh, I don't know. Something nice.'*

Nah, really?

You: *'Well, they like biking/cooking/eating their own nasal hair, what about we get them something from one of those cool gadgety catalogues or websites?'*

Him: *'Brilliant idea!'*

You: *'OK, I'll have a look and see what's new.'*

Him: *'Great!'*

And that's it! You have foolishly managed to turn the 'we' into 'I' and are now stuck with getting Christmas presents for all of his family for the rest of time. And will they even thank you for it? They will not. They will thank him for the presents, assuming, not unreasonably, that he had at least something to do with them as they are his relatives not yours. And will he thank you for it? Certainly not enough.

And don't forget it's not just Christmas – it's birthdays too. Now you have saddled yourself with the task of remembering the birthdays of all of the assorted brothers/sisters/parents/nephews etc. as well! And planning what to get, and posting the presents, and, and ...

Hang on.

Step back from the edge of the abyss.

CHRISTMAS PRESENT

You need to make sure this nightmare vision of Christmases to come doesn't happen. The first and best way of making sure of this is by never getting yourself into such a mess in the first place. Never have the 'What are we going to get for X?' conversation. Rather, be very strict with yourself: the question to ask instead is, 'What are *you* going to get for X?' Or better still, never have that conversation. Talk about what presents you are getting for *your* brother/sister/decrepit uncle etc. and see if he can join the dots in his own mind to his own family.

It helps very much if presents arrive at your house sent by his family in the post (posted by a female of that family, presumably, and usually), as you can point at them and say things like 'Oh, look at the lovely presents that have arrived from your X' (not from his ex, that would be a very bad thing indeed), and suggest he puts them under the tree.

CHRISTMAS PRESENT (ROUND 2)

If, as is likely, you have fallen into what Frank Sinatra memorably called 'the tender trap' of buying his presents for him, then the task is how to get yourself out of it. I'm afraid I only have one answer, and it is one that won't be very popular with him, or with his family, but it is the only solution: cold turkey. Way before Boxing Day.

Mid-December you have to launch the bombshell that you are not buying his Christmas presents for him this year. I'm not suggesting you just come out and say that, of course! (Ha ha, the very idea of just coming out and saying it!) No, you can either use the subtle approach, or the outright lie.

THE SUBTLE APPROACH

The subtle approach is that you just stop using 'we' language and start using 'you' language and hope for the best:

You: *'What are you going to get for blah for Christmas this year?' [Spoken with innocence in your voice but with no eye contact.]*

Him: *'Errr …' [Watch as the panic sets in.]*

Repetition is now essential, and eye contact is permissible, but you must be prepared for the look of horror/utter confusion in his eyes and not break down (either in your iron will, or into fits of giggles) in the face of it. Leave it a day and then broach the subject again:

You: *'Just remind me what you were going to get blah for Christmas this year?' [Then swiftly exit the scene, with a hurried 'Just got to pop out to—' and leave him in his semi-apoplectic state. And see what happens.]*

There is a small, but perceptible, chance that this may work. So it could be worth a go. But if you fear it will lead to more questions than answers, then I suggest that the outright lie is for you.

THE OUTRIGHT LIE

No matter what your economic circumstances, or the global situation, you can always find some kind of justification in any given year since time began for the following statement: 'I think we ought to have an austerity Christmas this year.'

This is a genius masterstroke that cannot fail. It doesn't matter at all if you actually follow this through (unlikely) or if you fail to observe it completely, *other than* to fail to buy any of 'his' presents. All you need to do is follow it up with: 'So, I don't think I'll get anything for your side of the family, you know, from *me*. Of course, if you want to go ahead and get them something from you, then that's fine.'

Once husband has fully absorbed what you are saying, he will realize that – as long as you do not flinch and buy them something last minute, which you mustn't – he will have to pull his finger out or suffer the wrath of his family. The probable outcome of your move is that half of them won't get anything this year, hence your unpopularity with them as they now realize that it was you who got their presents all along. Trust me, this won't result in their thanking you for this post hoc, and it will result in them resenting you a tiny bit. But the precedent will have been set and they will have forgotten by the New Year anyway.

Your boots are no longer on the ground of this battlefield, and so any problems his family have with their lack of presents are not your problems. You have won the PR war of presents.

THE GIFT OF GIVING

Now you have also given him back the gift of giving – ahh, smiley face. He will thank you for it in the long run. OK, he won't thank you for it, but at least you won't have to buy all those Christmas and birthday presents for his family year after sodding year, and that's the main thing.

As I say, this masterplan does not at all mean that you have to actually have an austerity Christmas. And when you chatter about how you have bought so-and-so such a lovely doo-dah, bit expensive but lovely, and he says the inevitable, 'But I thought we were having an austerity Christmas!', you simply reply, 'Well, yes, I did start off with just little presents, but John Lewis has such lovely things this year ...'

And if it turns out that he carries through with the austerity Christmas theory, in the form of a present to you from Poundland ... Don't worry, that's what the January sales are for.

Top Tip

Of course, one of the difficulties is that sometimes there may be presents you like choosing, buying and giving. It's almost Munchausen's syndrome by proxy in the form of retail therapy. It's such fun choosing those cute little playsuits for the nieces! And it's nice to buy posh kitchen stuff for the brother-in-law, even if you do have to actually give it to him. But you *must* resist this temptation! Otherwise that's it, for ever. You will be Mother Christmas for all of your family and friends, and for all of his family too (not friends, obviously – he doesn't have many of those, and he certainly doesn't give any of them presents). Be strong.

Learning to talk

We all like to think the human race is distinct, that we are pure *Homo sapiens*. But if we look into our DNA we will see that in our past ancestry we all slept with Neanderthals – I know I have! And nowhere is this heritage clearer than in the language that we often find our boys talking, before we have weaned them off their Neanderthal language the Contented way.

Fortunately, the Contented method is here to help you grow your boy's developing language skills and help him to master more and more complicated vocabulary and leave the Neanderthal stage of his life behind him.

REVERSING LANGUAGE REGRESSION

The first step to helping your boy to increase his language

skills is in understanding that he has needed to use these unfortunate and inappropriate language terms in order to fit in with his previous important others – this is to say, the bunch of Neanderthals he used to hang around with. So the language was used as a form of identity. But now he has a new identity: being your husband. And once you have managed to get rid of his primitive buddies dragging him down, you will be able to tackle the language too. It is important to understand that while the language was a form of belonging, it was also a regression to early, more basic forms of communication, and so what you need to do is reverse this language regression.

NEANDERTHAL LANGUAGE EXPLAINED

Classic examples of Neanderthal language:

- slash
- gut
- dump

As you can see, much early language is monosyllabic and concerned with body parts and bodily functions. This is inevitable, as Neanderthal language is at an earlier stage of development than grown-up human language. So, for example, the Neanderthal phrase 'Man, my gut is killing me' is easily translated as 'I have a stomach ache'. This alternative is clearly preferable, as it is readily understood and has the added advantage of being acceptable in polite society.

HABIT REVERSAL

How to change his language is now the question. While this area of language development has been unaccountably ignored by academic literature, I have found that an overlapping body of research can be successfully applied to help solve this problem. Habit reversal is the first approach to try. This is actually a pretty simple process that uses a combination of praise and discipline which is not unlike that of training a dog. The vital difference here is of offers of beer taking the place of Scooby Snacks. The training goes like this:

Him: *'I'm going for a slash/dump/etc.'*

You [acting confused]: *'Sorry? Did you say you were going to the toilet?'*

Him: *'Yes that's right, that's what I said. I am going to the toilet.'*

You: *'Ah, OK. I understand! Well, I've got a cold beer ready for you when you get back!'*

There is a slight risk that he will begin to associate his use of inappropriate language with offers of lager on ice, but that is just a risk you will have to take, I'm afraid. Hey, no one said this was easy – you can't make an omelette without breaking dishes, you know. Or at least I can't.

COMPREHENSIVE BEHAVIOURAL INTERVENTION

If you find that the habit reversal approach does not work, or even that it backfires horribly, then the only hope for you is Comprehensive Behavioural Intervention. It's not as scary as it sounds, don't worry. Well, actually it is. What you are looking at here is basically entirely reprogramming his brain. You may think it's not worth doing this for the sake of a few bits of Neanderthal language, and I have to say you're probably right.

So alternatively, why not just shout at him: 'Could you stop telling me you're going for a dump please, it's horrible!'

See if that works. I don't know, sometimes I just about give up.

Contentment? Who needs it.

Top Tip

There are examples of successful use of dog clicker training to habit reverse Neanderthal language. But it's so demeaning that even I can't sanction its use.

I just can't.

Weaning

Bringing your lovely boy out into the world is a heavy responsibility. So you had better make sure he is a credit to you when he is out and about. You may not mind that his language is at an early stage of development, and that he wants to make friends with the bully of the playgroup, but your friends and acquaintances certainly will. So if you want to stay on the invite list for your cool friends' parties, you had better make sure your boy is fully house-trained and socially acceptable before unleashing him upon them. The issue here is how to wean him off unsuitable friends and unacceptable language. It's not that *all* his friends are awful, there are just some that leave a bit to be desired …

WEANING – FACING THE PROBLEM

You know the ones I mean – some are crashing bores, some are amazing dweebs and some are just the ones that style, grace and subtlety left behind. And your sweetheart needs to move on and leave them behind too. But that's fine, he doesn't need all his friends any more – he has you and, if he behaves well enough, your friends too. But how to wean him off those dreadful childhood, and still frankly adolescent, friends?

It's important that you never tackle this issue head on. Do not say what you actually think! Never ever, under any circumstances, should you say something along the lines of:

'Oh my God, I cannot bear another evening with sodding Marvin and Eric and that crowd. They are some of the most incredible dimwits I have ever had the misfortune to meet, who seem to think that a good night out literally consists of nothing but standing up drinking beer, then sitting down and eating curry ad infinitum. Dear Christ, is that what we were brought on this planet to achieve? Is that why our ancestors crawled out of the primeval soup? Is this what Galileo and Marie Curie died for? Is this literally IT?'

Don't say that. Or anything even a bit close to that. Don't even say something like:

'Do you know, I am not sure I really like Marvin and Eric that much. I think they might be more to your taste than mine. That's OK with you, isn't it?'

Attitudes like this will merely serve to drive a wedge between you and your best boy, and that's no good for anyone. And it's certainly no good for getting you invited to dinner parties! You need a date for many social occasions – why would you have made so much effort improving your boy's hair and wardrobe otherwise? – but you need to be able to trust that he will behave properly and respectfully.

It is vitally important that you wean him off his old unsuitable friends but you must certainly not risk the direct approach of telling him you don't like them, or asking him not to see them so much now that you two are together. So how is the deed to be done?

KILL WITH KINDNESS

'I come not to bury Caesar but to praise him': the strategy you need is that instead of criticizing his friends, you must praise them. Overpraise them! Say things that are so wildly implausible and most certainly untrue about their many and unrivalled virtues that at some point the penny will drop in your boy's developing brain and he will realize that his friends really can't have any hope of living up to your claims for them. After this it is then another leap for him to realize that the people who do actually possess some of these noble qualities are, guess who ... *your* friends!

So, you need to have a conversation along the following lines:

You: *'You know, I was thinking should we get together with some of your friends from school? It's always so fun seeing them and finding out what they are getting up to.'*

He won't be expecting this, so immediately you will have caught him off-guard, which is just where you want him.

Him: *'Er, sure – great! How about we go to the pub?'*

Here comes your follow-up. You have already had them over for dinner a while ago – a ghastly evening of loud, boring conversation and wholesale destruction of your drinks cabinet. But it was worth it, for this comeback:

You: *'Well, isn't it X's turn to have everyone round for dinner? It was such a good evening when they were all over here for dinner that I'm sure everyone will want to do that again. And I bet that X is a brilliant cook – I can't wait to see what he will whip up in the kitchen with those huge fish he catches every weekend.'*

Him: *'Really?'*

You: *'Oh yes. And of course Z has an incredible eye for fashion so we have superbly interesting conversations about the latest fashion moods.'*

Fashion moods? Don't worry that it doesn't actually make sense or mean anything, it's all part of the mystification process.

And you have mystified him. He is now seriously confused. Are these the same friends that he knows all too well? They sound amazing! But scary. And so scared will he be of the vision of this encounter that you have just set out that, strangely, the dinner party at X's house will never happen. And while it never happens, it would be bad form of him to meet up with them at the pub and deprive you of their allegedly scintillating company. And instead there is a dinner party at your friends' house, and suddenly you both need to be there instead. And now he realizes that he needs to know how to make conversation about modern architectural trends and the latest vogues, and so in desperation he will actually pick up those achingly trendy magazines you have been leaving around the house, and soon Marvin and Eric will be but distant memories.

Friends he used to have before he met you.

Just as it should be.

CAN'T I JUST KEEP ONE ...?

Of course, you may decide that you actually like some of his friends. In which case, of course they are keepers, no problem. Equally, you may decide that while you intensely dislike all of his friends, one or two of them can occasionally serve useful purposes, and most certainly, the Contented approach to life would often suggest this (I refer you to the useful purpose Eric serves in the 'Understanding man flu' section in Chapter 5). You may also find it useful for him to have a buddy to go off on surfing weekends with or to sit next to in the freezing cold at a rugby match, so that you can spend the day at that spa you really wanted to go to but couldn't justify the expense until he went off for a weekend surfing. And so with this in mind, and possibly also to show your lovely boy how very much you care for him, you may think to leave him with at least *one* friend who you find socially acceptable, and who doesn't make you roll your eyes when he says that he is meeting up with them.

Meanwhile, you can assuage any guilt you may feel by reminding yourself that you are being cruel only to be kind – these old friends of his are not good for him. Those badly behaved kids are a bad influence. When he's with them he stays up too late, he drinks the nice bottles of Sancerre you had pegged for an evening for you both together, he bets on the horses and he talks in a seemingly serious way about going out to the dogs track to watch the races. You are only acting in his best interests.

AVERSION THERAPY

But if killing with kindness has not worked and his friends are still the bane of your life, then you are just going to have to use aversion therapy. I am sorry if this is the case as it's not really a whole lot of fun, for either of you. But if Eric and Marvin are still featuring heavily in his and your life, and destroying all hope you had of having a well-mannered boy you can take out with you, then there is nothing for it but this. There is only one way of carrying out aversion therapy against his friends, and that is by the following method. I warn you that you won't read this method in any of the nanny state 'self-help' books out there today, as they have all sorts of objections to it (using negative words like 'appalling'), but if you still want to proceed, it's up to you. I'm not saying that I suggest it, I am just letting you know what the therapy is. Whether or not you use it can be nothing to do with me. I'm just the conduit and I can't be blamed for that, can I. Can I?

Well, at your own risk, here it is.

Get him very drunk one evening, you a bit less drunk, and then without him realizing what you are doing show him a photo of one of his friends, and just when he is about to say 'Why are you showing me—' give him a smart punch on the arm. 'Hey, what was that for?' he will shout, not unreasonably. 'Oh, sorry!' you reply. Then change the conversation for a few minutes, ply him with another drink until he has forgotten the smart punch on the arm, then follow with a different friend and get a pointy stick to work on a different bit of him. Of course, be careful not to actually hurt him at any point – no one wants that!

Psychologists call this 'positive punishment', with the photo of his friends providing the 'aversive stimulus'. Photo of his friend = prod with pointy stick. Thus his friend = pain (which you've been saying all along).

I did warn you it was an unpleasant treatment. But it is effective as a last resort. You may need to repeat the process, possibly more than once, for the psychological change to take effect. And of course it is vital that you deny all knowledge of what happened in the morning. Ideally, he will not remember either. But instead it will have been imprinted on his impressionable brain that old friends equal pain. Which indeed they do!

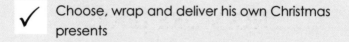

Progress report

By this point, your Contented Little Husband should be able to:

✓ Choose, wrap and deliver his own Christmas presents

✓ Use a more sophisticated vocabulary

✓ Make friends that you approve of

✓ Talk knowledgably about subjects other than his work or cars

5

THAT'S BETTER,
NO MORE TEARS

Travel tantrums

LOST IN WALES

You know the scene, only too well. You and darling husband are in a car, driving hopelessly up and down a country road in the middle of nowhere, usually in Wales, while the rain drums relentlessly and deafeningly on the roof of the car and the grey of the sky is matched only by the black of your moods. You have no signal on your mobile, and the satnav is also paralysed by the situation and is endlessly screaming out 'Recalculating! Recalculating!' like a crazed dalek. Any hope of ever finding the country cottage you were to spend an 'idyllic weekend' in, getting back to nature – all because 'darling husband' is too tight to fork out for a hotel in Paris, of course – is fading fast and you are just about to give it all up and start a new life as a travelling gypsy when suddenly you see it: salvation! An actual real person, certainly alive and definitely trudging miserably, but purposefully, through the rain with dog at heels and wellies suitably covered in mud. This person is clearly your knight in shining armour, for they are indisputably a local.

'Quick, we'll pull over and ask for directions!' you shout while manically applying the brakes.

'No, no,' comes back the immediate response from husband. 'Keep driving! I think we're nearly there. I'm sure that tree was in the photos of the directions.'

'Don't be insane! We've been going round in circles for the best part of an hour and this is the first actual person we've seen. I'm stopping and you can ask them for directions. They're on your side of the car. Quick, before they walk on past us!'

'NO, NO!' he replies, with genuine panic in his eyes. 'It's OK, I know what – I can get internet on my Kindle! Don't stop, don't stop! 'Cause if the Kindle doesn't work I'll just make a short-wave radio! We've got wires in the boot and can use the car radio antenna and—'

Frankly, he's babbling. You've stopped the car. You've

wound his window down and here comes said bedraggled individual approaching the car.

'Just ask him the way,' you say to your darling boy. *'It's not difficult.'*
'Are you two OK?' asks our pedestrian Good Samaritan, smiling pleasantly.
'Errr ...' says husband, turning to you.

Oh dear, deep sigh. You are literally going to have to do that thing. You are going to have to talk over your dearest

one almost as if he were invisible, or very much as if he were a small, helpless child ... and say those words that your darling boy just cannot bring himself to utter: 'We're lost. Please could you give us directions?'

Not so hard, is it? Eight words. Eight tiny little words. (OK, well, 'directions' is a bit of a long word but apart from that.)

And so our humble dishevelled hero tells us the way to the 'idyllic' cottage. Or rather, the hero tells *you*, as darling boy refuses to listen and spends the time staring intently at said Kindle instead, muttering something about how he was just about to suggest that route.

Oh dear. Is there ever a way to change this? Is there a way to give your darling boy the tools to make the hardest ask – learning how to ask for directions?

MUSIC THERAPY

If music be the food of love, sing on. And on. To the point beyond which he can bear it no more and breaks down in tears. Yes, organize your car-journey playlist to play and repeat songs with a helping theme and then sing along loudly to them. First up, of course, the classic 'Rescue Me'. Then Dionne Warwick's 'Do You Know the Way to San Jose?' And end up with the seminal 'Is This the Way to Amarillo?', a song about the only guy in history who is in fact able to ask for directions. Praise the lead character as a powerful male role model from whom we can learn such a lot, specifically about how to ask for directions.

THRIFTY THERAPY

We all know how much men hate wasting money, right? I mean on handbags and scarves and shoes, of course. But also on petrol. Many are the fascinating conversations I have had over the years about the price of petrol in different service stations ... And yet a recent survey by GPS manufacturer TrekAce found that men will drive on average an extra 900 miles in their lifetime while driving around lost. Think of the petrol money that equates to! Or rather, get your precious sweetheart to think about it. I find the best way of doing this is with something along the lines of the following conversation:

You: *'I'm just off to buy a new bottle of perfume. There's my favourite brand at the moment going for only £150.'*

Him: *'Only?!'*

You: *'It's OK – since I'm doing the driving from now on, I've worked out we will be saving that much by not driving around for an extra 900 miles.'*

Him: *'What on earth are you talking about?!'*

And then you explain. I'm not suggesting he will be happy with the explanation, but he will have to recognize its logic.

TIME IS MONEY

We all know how your darling values his time – he doesn't want to be bothered with straightening sheets on the bed or plumping up cushions; he doesn't have the time for that sort of nonsense. Well, wait till he finds out about this: a quarter of men spend thirty minutes being lost before they will ask for directions. The other three quarters spend longer, of course. So, I can recommend this approach:

You: *'Would you mind going round the house please, angel, and checking all the pictures are level and straightening those that aren't?'*

Him: *'Errr ... [He is obviously appalled at being asked to do this mind-numbingly dull task which he feels is entirely beneath him.] Gosh, sorry, sweetness, I really don't have time for that today before we head off to Bob's for the weekend. I'll try to get onto it soon.'*

Then comes your killer rejoinder:

You: *'It's OK, I've printed off the instructions and they're really foolproof so we'll be saving that thirty minutes.'*

Him: *'What thirty minutes?'*

Ah, you say. Well, you see ...

Top Tip

Playing One Direction music rarely helps for two reasons: first, their name suggests not so much asking for directions as ploughing on in the same direction in the face of all the evidence, precisely the behaviour we want to change. And second, it usually gets switched off before the end of the first song anyway.

Understanding man flu

USEFUL ADVICE ON HOW TO FAKE SYMPATHY

So, that awful time comes. You hear a sneeze from your bundle of joy, then an unnecessarily loud 'Darling, the box of tissues, please!' spoken at you in dramatic tones, and, oh dear, you have the unmistakeable signs of man flu. That dreaded occurrence destined to turn the next two or three days of your life into a living hell. Now, if he's genuinely ill I'm sure you'll happily make chicken soup and run to the pharmacy for him, but I'm pretty sure last time you had a sore throat you still managed to go to work and then cook dinner *and* do the laundry – know what I mean, ladies? Before you presume a case of man flu though, it is important to check your own instinctive wifely intuition with that of a fully trained professional. It's OK; as ever, I am here to help. To be sure of your initial diagnosis of man flu, you need to check for the following telltale signs.

COMMON SYMPTOMS OF MAN FLU

- No fever
- No unexpected or unexplained spots
- No visible paling or reddening of the skin
- General moping
- Extra loud coughing/sneezing when you are nearby

CONDITIONS INCREASING THE
LIKELIHOOD OF MAN FLU

- A birthday party of one of your friends or family coming up that he would definitely not like to go to
- No big sporting or music events coming up that he has tickets to
- Some boring house paperwork that needs to be done
- A slight drop in temperature accompanied by him forgetting to wear a jumper – once

One symptom that absolutely must be present to make a confident diagnosis of man flu: a total refusal to see a doctor.

If some or all of the symptoms are present, and if they are accompanied by the presence of a pitiful man dragging himself around the house complaining, 'I just don't have any energy at all,' then you can be sure that you have a classic case of man flu. Poor you. Having to deal with him in this state is guaranteed to be a whole heap of no fun. Of course, it's heartbreaking to see him in this state; it's awful seeing his little face looking up at you with such self-pitying hopelessness in his eyes, and, although of course he can't express it, you know he is thinking, 'How long will it be like this? How long until I am myself and can tear around the house again?' The answer to this is always two or three days, but of course it will seem like an eternity to him.

So here are some strategies for you to cope with this big baby until he finally gets off his arse and acts like a real man again. Choose the one that is best for you both and your particular relationship – hey, I'm not here to lecture you on how to live your life!

1. Mind games: the over-the-top approach

This is how it works: you see the first signs of the dreaded man flu and instantly go into overdrive: 'Oh no, you poor darling. I heard that sneeze – it sounded terrible! This could be really serious – shall I phone the surgery and see if I can make an appointment today?' This technique works in person, but it also works on the phone, e.g. if he has called you at work to let you know how dreadful he feels and how you need to drop everything you are doing to help/sympathize/make him a sandwich.

When he replies in the negative – that it isn't so bad and there's no need to worry – it is important that you meet this with a stiff rejoinder: 'But I *am* worried, darling! We can't have you being sick and not looked after, can we? If the surgery doesn't have an appointment today then I could look into getting an emergency doctor for you? It will probably cost about £100 but it's worth it to have you looked after.'

Don't worry about the potential expense of making this suggestion, as there's absolutely no chance at all that he will take you up on it. But do be careful – don't go too far: if you suggest you call an ambulance he will know for certain that you are taking the mick.

Upsides of this approach

In the best-case scenario, and I have known this to work with some absolute horrors who then became perfect angels, it can shut down man flu altogether. By which I mean that the sneezes continue, but the whining doesn't (he still whines, but now only to male colleagues and friends). If this approach doesn't get rid of man flu it may at least make him choose to suffer in relative silence. You might not be able to avoid totally the drama of him soldiering bravely on, but at least he may stop bothering you every three seconds with an update on his 'symptoms'.

Downside of this approach

It requires totally convincing acting to carry it off. If he picks up any hint that you aren't really worried, he will instantly become even more unbearable. To picture what I mean, imagine a toddler having a tantrum in the supermarket and substitute grown man for toddler, and you're getting close.

2. The 'best friend' approach: getting others to fake sympathy so you don't have to

This is a more subtle strategy. You may find it hard to make it work, but it is a real humdinger if you can pull it off. At the first sound of 'I feel so awful I can't face seeing anybody', you immediately go into full sympathy mode: 'How miserable for you. I totally understand. Of course, I'm sure it would do you good to have a pint with Eric [substitute best friend's name], but I can see how you can't face it.' Now, here comes the clever bit. He knows you don't like him having pints with Eric – why would you? Eric is a crashing bore. 'Noooo,' he says, 'I don't think I could face it.' Aha! Classic man flu! So you pick up the phone and beg Eric to come over and cheer up poor husband. ('No, don't worry, not contagious!' you reassure. Well it isn't, you see – it's man flu.)

Over comes Eric; husband fakes horror. Eric and husband have a drink. Husband laughs and is merry, but not too merry otherwise you will surely notice he's not so sick after all. Eric gives him three words of sympathy, if you can count 'Cheer up, mate' as sympathy. Eric leaves. Husband goes to sleep. It's all good.

Upsides of this approach

With minimal effort on your part, dear hubby is distracted enough to forget about his sniffles and instantly feels better. You and Eric bond over caring for the 'patient', and, to be honest, you really should make more of an effort to get to know Eric.

Downsides of this approach

No matter how hard you try, you really can't stand Eric.

3. The honest approach: tell him you think he's malingering and not really that sick

Never, never do this. Ever. I beg you. While satisfying to say, it's just not worth it.

> *Top Tip*
>
> If gentle management like this doesn't work then there is a chance he really is feeling rotten. One unmistakable sign of this is that he lets you take charge of the remote control when watching TV. In this case, now is the time to spoil him. Stroke his forehead, tuck him in and give him lots of sympathy and affection – and be sure to make a mental note and remind him of this next time you're ill.

Your first time away

DECOY PRICING

To paraphrase a well-known self-help book, men like Mars bars and women like holidays in Venice. The issue is holidays and how to get them.

To start off with, you know about decoy pricing, right? You may think you don't, but if you have ever bought popcorn in a cinema or a drink from a high-street café chain, you have experienced decoy pricing.

There you are in a well-known café on your local high street, deciding not to worry about the massive sugar content of a hot chocolate and ordering one. But which size to get? The small costs £2.50, the regular is 80p more at £3.30, while the large is then only a tiny bit more again at £3.50. What to do?

Well, you start thinking that you will get the small, to be virtuous in saving money and reducing sugar. But it is very small, the small ... So you look at the regular, and that has a lot more chocolate and for not that much more money. And then that makes you look at the large – this is even more chocolately, but for only a little more money than the regular. So you go for it. You order the large. And it is only as you waddle away with a veritable bucket of hot milk, chocolate and sugar swilling around inside you that you realize that you had only planned to have the small. So how did you end up supersizing up to the large? It was the cheeky regular that did it. Its poor value made the large look like good value, and we can't resist a 'bargain'. The regular was the decoy.

AND NOW FOR THE HOLIDAYS

But what does this have to do with you getting yourself the holidays you want, I hear you cry? Well, it's all about the decoy. Now you understand how it works, here's what you can do.

Your aim: lovely holiday in Italy – villa with pool, near the sea, lots of sun, sand, nice wine, good food, shopping in quaint cobbled streets. Cost: £1,000.

His aim: holiday in a pub. Cost: £90 plus £30 for the kebabs.

How are you to bridge this gap? This is how.

You: *'I've been thinking about our summer holiday. [He groans, fearing both the conversation and the implied cost.] And I was wondering if we could do something a bit different this year?'*

Him: *'Right … Such as what?'*

You: *'Well, I've thought of a few options. We could do something really cheap [his face brightens at the sound of this], like we could stay at my friend's uncle's cottage in Scotland?'*

Obviously a terrible idea, and he knows it, but you have to make sure its immense cheapness doesn't mean it wins out in his mind. So you have to follow up with: 'Although, it looks like the uncle is actually going to be there this year and so we would have to sleep on the sofabed in the lounge, but even so, it's a thought. What do you think?'

Him: *'No, we're not that broke – we can afford to do our own thing. What about a staycation? We could go to a pub!'*

Don't even bother to reply to that, just move straight on to the decoy. But be aware that he has given away a vital point – you can afford to do your own thing. So off you go!

You: *'Well in that case, I wondered about camping at a bee farm. I have found a super place which offers good deals if you don't mind sharing tents – it's only £800 for the week. I mean, the weather might not be brilliant as they are mountainous bees, we can't choose who we would share a tent with and I'm not sure there's really that much to do there, but what do you think?'*

Obviously, he will think this is the worst deal that anyone has ever been offered anywhere. As indeed it is! Particularly if he is allergic to bee stings. So before you give him any time to reply, move straight on to the choice you want him to buy – the large popcorn, the bucket of hot chocolate, the supersize option, which in this case is, guess what:

You: *'Or for just a leetle bit more I have found a lovely villa in Italy, near the sea, and ever such a pretty town with great restaurants [don't mention the shopping], and with flights and everything all in. It's only a bit more than the bee place. Maybe we should go for that?'*

Him: *'Well, that does seem better value ...'*

And so, the job is done.

WE'RE ALL GOING ON A SUMMER HOLIDAY!

Soon you will be winging your way to bella Italia, and he will eventually realize that the phrase 'with everything all in' did not include the meals or the wine, let alone the shopping. But it will be too late by then. You will soon be back home, working out how to pay the credit card bill and planning the next holiday.

Now that's what I call contentment.

HOLIDAY BLUES

Once the holiday is booked you aren't entirely out of the woods. There is also the small matter of enjoying the holiday. There are many aspects to this minefield. It begins with the packing: you may want to prepare in advance and pack things you will actually need. He wants to shove a T-shirt and swimmies in a bag and say, 'We can buy anything else we need when we're out there.' The only successful defence I have found against this obvious act of lazy idiocy is to remark that it will all add to the cost of the holiday (as if that wasn't bleeding obvious) and maybe it would make more sense to save the euros for fun stuff, like a nice dinner or kite-surfing.

And then there's the question of what you will both actually do on the holiday. Perhaps you are both keen cyclists and will merrily pedal along on a tandem together. Or perhaps you both want to go on a Motörhead cruise ship (yes they do exist, I am not making this up). In which case, bully for you. Aren't you both going to be happy campers. Maybe you both even enjoy camping.

Or maybe there will be a bit of a disconnect. Maybe you will like floating serenely around markets and boutique shops, searching for the ideal treasures to bring back home. Treasures that he will call overpriced tat. Maybe he wants to stay up too late drinking the local grog so that he never wants to get up and see anything, let alone do anything, before lunch by which time it's too hot to move. Or maybe he wants to spend each day doing that kite-surfing and you, well, don't. Yes, it's not all plain sailing, unless you are on that Motörhead cruise. What to do?

You could compromise. You could each take it in turns to choose the holiday and all that goes into it. But there is an obvious flaw to this argument: you would then have to actually follow through with it. Holiday in the pub here we come ... I think not.

So instead, you could *pretend* to compromise!

You: *'I know, darling, let's have this holiday be my choice, and then we can see what we think for the next holiday. What do you think?'*

It's sneaky but it might just work. The strategy can be summed up as 'keep kicking the can down the road for literally ever'. You just have to be aggressive with that decoy each and every holiday time. I know, it's tough. Hey, no one said Contentment was easy.

If there is only one piece of advice you take from this chapter, let it be this: never, ever say, 'I used to go on such great holidays with my ex-boyfriend. Why can't you be more like him?'

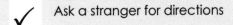

Progress report

By this point, your Contented Little Husband should be able to:

✓ Ask a stranger for directions

✓ Suffer man flu in relative silence

✓ Imagine a holiday that does not involve a pub

✓ Pack a suitcase without assistance

6

COMMON PROBLEMS SOLVED

In this chapter we take a metaphorical baby wipe to a host of problems commonly faced by discontented wives, and with a swish of this antibacterial cloth, we will clear up the whole mess. Or at least as much of it as is humanly possible. I mean, some things are simply not achievable. For example:

HOW CAN I GET HIM TO REMEMBER MY BIRTHDAY OR OUR ANNIVERSARY?

If I knew the answer to this, my friend, I would be a millionaire.

MY HUSBAND APPEARS TO BE ON TWITTER TWENTY-FIVE HOURS A DAY. HOW CAN I STOP THIS?

You can't. Be realistic. The best you can hope for is that he occasionally uses it for professional purposes. Look on the bright side – getting hold of him is just a tweet away.

MY HUSBAND STOPPED GOING TO THE GYM WHEN WE GOT MARRIED – WHY DOES HE THINK I NO LONGER CARE WHAT HE LOOKS LIKE?

It's not that he thinks you don't care what he looks like any more, instead it's that he never really considered whether you cared what he looked like; he knew that when he was single, he had to keep up appearances to find a mate. Now that he has a mate his efforts have to go not on keeping in shape for your sake, but rather in becoming as large a physical presence as possible so as to substantiate the claim that he is king of the jungle (with you as his queen). Hence the lack of gym work. And the increase in pies.

Just make sure you take some nice photos of him in the early years so you can remember how good he looked before the love handles set in.

WHY DOES MY HUSBAND THINK IT'S OK TO DRESS THE WAY HE DOES?

A common problem. The answer is not just that he has never prioritized dress sense (except again during the period when he was searching for a mate), the answer goes deeper than that: he thinks it is rather suspect to have good dress sense. It smacks of trying to please too much, of conforming to the Man, of being part of the capitalist oligarchy. Plus, more honestly, it's much easier just to sling on the first clothes his hands touch in the chest of drawers. Never mind if your eighty-year-old grandmother is coming round and might not appreciate that T-shirt slogan. In a nutshell, he thinks it's OK to be pretty lazy about a whole bunch of things. Be glad if you're only complaining about his dress sense.

However, before you break down in despair at the futility of trying to change your boy's bad behaviour and wonder why you committed yourself to this monster in the first place, fear not – other problems are much more manageable, if not completely curable (see below).

WHY DOES MY HUSBAND LEAVE HIS DIRTY CLOTHES ON THE FLOOR ALL THE TIME? DOES HE NOT LOVE ME?

I know it seems to make no sense, but he does love you really, even though he leaves his dirty clothes all over the floor rather than in the washing basket. I find that the best solution to this problem is a few weeks of the lowest form of wit – sarcasm – in the following form: 'Oh dear,' you say while picking up a particularly egregious sock between extended forefinger and thumb, 'Could this not make it on its own to the washing basket? Poor thing.' He will not appreciate your tone, but he might realize he ought to do better. If this fails, the next step is to simply pick up his dirty clothes from the floor and place them in his clean clothes drawers. The only problem with this strategy is that he will often not notice, and even if he does he may not care. If this is the case, there is little that can be done, sadly.

But if – oh joy! – he does notice the swapsies and doesn't like them, then you are well on the way to a solution. Now all you need to do is to find some excuse in the bathroom layout to install two washing baskets: one for your things, one for his. When yours is full you empty it, and wash and dry the contents. And when his is full, it is his job to do the same. Not your job. If you make it your job to begin with, you may never escape the role. And you will be there in thirty years' time picking up his dirty clothes from the floor and washing, drying and delivering to him perfectly folded clothes, about which he cares almost not a jot. That is not the future I have in mind for you. So start making this his responsibility now – or else!

WHY DOES MY HUSBAND NOT KNOW THAT WET TOWELS WILL MAKE OTHER THINGS WET IF PUT ON TO THEM? DOES HE NOT UNDERSTAND PHYSICS?

It seems very confusing, doesn't it – the delight of your life professes to understand complicated bits of science such as how electricity works, and what the Large Hadron Collider is for, and yet he seems not to understand the principle of osmosis: that water in an item, such as a wet towel, will transfer in a relatively short time to a dry item, such as a clean, freshly made bed, if put on top of it. Unfortunately, this is a well-known phenomenon whereby academic learning fails to be applied in real-life situations. Another way of summarizing the effect is booksmart vs streetsmart. One example of the phenomena is his understanding of complex security systems, but his inability to remember his keys.

The best way of countering this behaviour is by taking the activity back up to the level of an academic matter, a matter on which you wish to defer to him – after all, he is always right. Enter into an engaged and stimulating debate on the question of precisely how much water would be transferred to the fresh bed linen by the soggy towel, and how would one measure this. Jolly interesting, don't you know. At the end of this lengthy and extremely tedious debate there is a small chance that he has got the point that you don't want the sodding wet towel on the sodding dry bed.

Of course, if he nevertheless still hasn't realized this then you have to try a different tack, more along the lines of: 'What sort of moron are you? Can't you understand that your soggy towel is making our nice dry duvet cover horrible and wet?' That usually gets results. Not necessarily the results we want, but results of a sort. And we can't always ask for more than that.

WHY DOES MY HUSBAND MAN-LOOK FOR THINGS AND NEVER FIND THEM?

Ah, man-looking. That process of walking round in circles saying, 'Where is it? Where is it?' while flapping his arms about, not lifting anything up or looking underneath it. It is of course never successful in finding anything, but then it never aims to be; the aim instead is to seem to be such a helpless, panicked creature that *you* will be overcome with sympathy and empathy and find it for him.

This is why he calls out, 'Where is my x?' assuming that you will know where it is, with the clear implication that it is your job to find it. It is invariably this question that is called out, rather than the neutral alternative: '*Do you know* where my x is?', which gives you the option to answer with a simple 'No'. The only successful way I have found for making this linguistic shift is by a series of answers along the lines of: 'I don't know where *your* x is, but it's probably wherever you left it,' followed by you making no attempt whatsoever to help him look for it.

Some studies have found that by a cruel trick of nature men genuinely can't see the things they're looking for. Apparently, we have superior colour vision and wider peripheral vision, which men haven't needed to develop as their tunnel vision is what they've always needed for hunting.

Now, I can't speak for all men, but I know my husband's hunting days are well behind him (by a couple of thousand years or so), so that's really no excuse any more.

WHEN MY HUSBAND SAYS HE DOESN'T NOTICE MESS, CAN THIS ACTUALLY BE TRUE?

It seems remarkable, and I know this isn't what you want to hear, but it can genuinely often be true. The angel of your heart might actually not notice the mess, and even if he does vaguely have an awareness of it he may simply not care. If this is different from your standpoint on the situation then you have a problem. But whatever you do, make sure you don't decide on a tactic of 'I won't vacuum for a while and see how long it is before he decides the floor is just too foul and reaches for the Hoover himself.' You could be a long, long time waiting.

To tackle a messy husband, I've found it effective to put things away for him. Obviously, I'm not talking about putting them away in sensible places that are helpful for him. Oh no. He insists on leaving dirty socks on the floor? Into his briefcase they go. He repeatedly kicks his shoes off in the middle of the hallway? Into the shed they go. Have fun with it – be creative. When he inevitably can't find any of his things (see man-looking, page 117) and asks where they are, shrug and say the mess was driving you crazy but you just can't remember where you put them … He'll soon learn it's much easier to just put things away himself than leave it up to you.

WHY DOES MY HUSBAND THINK IT'S OK TO FIX HIS TOYS, SUCH AS OILY BIKE CHAINS, IN THE LIVING ROOM?

An inability to recognize the correct location for certain activities is a common problem – e.g. farting in the bedroom, clipping toenails in the kitchen and mending his toys in the sitting room. The difficulty here is that if you have an actual man shed in the garden then his duty is clear – to remove his oily toys to that secure environment and crack on. If, however, budget and space was tight and you opted for a man drawer then you have only yourself to blame, as he simply doesn't have the space to play. In this case the options are: try to get him to squeeze his bicycle/ motorbike/ keyboard transformer or whatever into the drawer. Unlikely. Or find a sudden emergency makeshift man shed, such as the bit of patio at the front of the house by the bus stop.

The frustrating thing is that he already knows the correct location for these activities, and is willfully ignoring the rules. It is in times like this that I call upon my friend the naughty step, which in this case is the top rung of a ladder. Ask him to go up the ladder for a piece of unspecified DIY and then when he reaches the top reveal that he is simply there to take some time out on his own and consider the negative impact of his actions (i.e. getting oil all over the sitting room). For this to work, it is imperative that you are consistent. A warning is followed by a calm explanation of why he had to spend some time on the naughty step (of the ladder). Once he is ready to apologize, and you are ready to let him come down, give him lots of cuddles and a cold beer so he knows you still love him.

Controversial maybe, but it does the trick.

HOW TO DEAL WITH COMMON TYPES: BATHROOM REFUSERS, SNORERS, TOTAL CULTURE REFUSERS

We all know the scenario: perhaps he won't wash as frequently as he should, he snores or point blank refuses to engage in anything smacking of culture. Urgh, he sounds awful. I can only assume he's good in bed to make up for all that. I'm afraid that dealing with these afflictions is a serious undertaking and requires a whole book dedicated to them alone.

HOW CAN I GET MY DIY DAMN WELL DONE?

There is a very common problem experienced by many people with their darling husbands, which can be summed up in just three little dreaded letters – DIY. The problem is simple: there is always mountains of it that needs doing, but no volunteers for actually doing it. But fear not, there is a solution to this thorny problem. Often darling husbands only find time to get round to doing the glamorous bits of DIY – the huge mirror in the sitting room that all the guests see: 'Oh gosh, what a beautiful mirror, that must have been quite a task to get it on the wall!' say visitors. 'Yes,' replies husband, smiling obscenely proudly, 'I put it up there myself.' 'And what a stunning fireplace – did you have that designed?' 'Well, yes and no,' says husband, in an attempt at humour. 'It was designed – but by me!' Yes, you remember that time well; there was talk of little else week after week as the entire house was filled with dust.

Meanwhile, unhung pictures are stacked on the floor, books are piling up needing shelves, lightbulbs are never changed as the house slowly descends into a Soviet era-style darkness, rooms still feature the old manky paint which was on the walls when you moved in, the woodwork is so tired and old that the colour has entirely shifted from the white it once was to some colour more akin to mouldy cream ... I could go on (and often do). Something has to be done.

But never, never, are you going to do that most dreaded of things to get it done – 'nag' him. If we have to ask for something to be done, and husband agrees to do it but never gets round to it, why should it be that we are criticized for 'nagging' him when we are simply pointing out he hasn't done it, and asking if he could see his way to do so? But nagging is what it is called. And this has to be avoided at all costs. So how, if he won't get round to it, and you don't want to pay a builder, are all the little unglamorous DIY tasks to get done?

My honest suggestion is that you Do It Your Goddamn Self. Most DIY, like putting up pictures, mirrors or curtain rails, is not hard, really it's not. And in many ways it's actually pretty good fun. Give yourself a head start by equipping yourself with a few vital tools of the trade, so often eschewed by our darling angels for being namby-pamby. Yes, start off by getting yourself an electric screwdriver. These are very cheap these days, their batteries last for ages, and they make the job of screwing in screws need no muscle power and take just a couple of seconds. You will also quite possibly have one over on your man with this purchase, as we all know that 'real men don't use electric screwdrivers'. Or at least, many of them appear to have a bizarre addiction to screwing things in by hand, because it 'gives more control' or some other such nonsense. Whereas in reality, all it actually gives you is less time to do other DIY tasks ... and an aching arm.

Why not get your own drill, rather than using 'his' (how come the drill is his, but the washing machine is yours?). Having your own has the crucial advantage that you will always know where it is – because you will have put it back in the correct place. With an electric screwdriver and your own drill, the only extra tool you need is a good strong hammer, plus some good strong nails, and attitude. With these vital components you are equipped to tackle most straightforward DIY tasks. You can put up coat racks, shelves and curtain rails without need of a single recourse to darling husband and his strength, 'expertise' or tools. And you can laugh in the face of that arduous task which he has been putting off for month after month.

From DIY hell to DIY heaven – it's easy when *you* do it.

WHY DOES MY HUSBAND FORGET EVERY SINGLE FAMILY CELEBRATION AND HOW CAN I CHANGE THIS?

Look, I'm not a miracle worker, OK? He forgets family celebrations because he doesn't care about them, and he also forgets them because he knows that *you* will remember. If you start not remembering things then maybe he will have to, just like he did in those years before he met you and abdicated responsibility for his relationships with friends and family.

WHY DOES MY HUSBAND NEVER ORGANIZE ANYTHING SO I HAVE TO DO IT ALL INSTEAD?

Or to put it another way, you do it all. It is not clear that you have to do so, just that you *do* do so. So – stop. Stop buying theatre tickets for you both to go to the theatre, and stop organizing dinner parties with friends at your house. Instead, organize things for yourself and girlfriends and wait until he notices. It may take a while but at some point he will spot that you're always off out at fun things while he is at home, hopefully doing the washing. And then, he will start to organize things for himself and for you too, just like he used to do back when you were dating and he was still going to the gym ...

MY HUSBAND COMPARED ME UNFAVOURABLY TO HIS MOTHER ONCE. SHOULD I FORGIVE HIM FOR THIS?

Absolutely not. Never. My advice is to keep bringing this up to make sure it never happens again. Ever. Whatever you do, don't let bygones be bygones.

EPILOGUE

SO NOW THAT HUBBY IS HAPPILY DOING ALL THE CHORES, WHAT TO DO WITH YOUR FREE TIME?

Why not take up hang gliding? And how about quad-bike racing? That's really fun. I can also thoroughly recommend surfing, especially in exotic foreign spots. There's also plenty to do nearer home, or even in it. Why not curl up with a good box set and a cuppa? While you're whiling away the hours happily watching a gripping drama, or trawling the internet for videos of cats, you can rest safe in the knowledge that hubby is at home, stacking the dishwasher, folding clothes and putting them away, beaming all the while with a happy, Contented smile.

Is this for real?

No, of course it isn't. And nor should it be. I bet your husband is a super chap who does loads of the cooking. I bet you share the daily chores of washing clothes and vacuuming floors. I bet you discuss your holiday wishes openly and honestly and have the same attitude to spending money. I am sure all you had to do was ask your husband once to put the loo seat down, and that was that. I hope that you already share your life together contentedly and have no need of any relationship advice from anyone.

EPILOGUE

But just in case there is a teeny weeny, tiny winy bit of truth in any of the diatribes in the book, please remember this: turtles make great pets and are much easier to train than husbands.

ACKNOWLEDGEMENTS

Huge thanks are due to all the many, many friends who helped make this book possible, most especially Vicky Prezeau, Kerrin Isaacs, Natasha Gardiner, Gisele Edwards and Amy Langley. Other friends are also totes great and all, but these ones actually helped with the book.

ABOUT THE AUTHOR

Tess Read lives in Exeter with three children, three turtles and one husband. They are all violently happy. And the turtles are certainly contented.